JOAN OF ARC

Heroine of France

by Ann Tompert
Illustrated by Michael Garland

Boyds Mills Press

The publisher wishes to thank Dr. Robert Shaffern,
Dr. Roy Domenico, and Rosemarie Pryle of the History Department
of the University of Scranton for their help in reviewing the manuscript.

Published by Boyds Mills Press, Inc.
A Highlights Company
815 Church Street
Honesdale, Pennsylvania 18431
Printed in China
Visit our Web site at www.boydsmillspress.com

Publisher Cataloging-in-Publication Data (U.S)

Tompert, Ann.
Joan of Arc: heroine of France / by Ann Tompert ; illustrations by Michael Garland. —
1st ed.
[32] p. : col. Ill. ; cm.
Summary: A brief biography of Joan of Arc, from her childhood to her martyrdom.
ISBN 1-59078-009-4
1. Joan, of Arc, Saint, 1412–1431 —- Juvenile literature. 2. Christian
women saints—France—Biography—Juvenile literature. 3. France—History—Charles VII,
1422–1461—Juvenile literature. (1. Joan, of Arc, Saint, 1412–1431.
2. Saints. 3. Women—Biography.) I..Garland, Michael. II. Title.
944/.026/ 092 B 21 CIP 2003
2002105797

First edition, 2003
The text of this book is set in 15-point Usherwood Medium.

10 9 8 7 6 5 4 3 2 1

For Jan, who said it couldn't be done
—A. T.

To my uncle Terry
—M. G.

They called her Joan the Maid. She lived more than five hundred years ago in the village of Domremy, France. Her parents, Jacques and Isabelle d'Arc, were peasant farmers. Like most peasant children, Joan helped to plow and hoe the fields and guard the sheep and cattle in the meadow. She did not go to school.

"It was from my mother I learned my prayers," she said. "She taught me to spin and sew."

All was not work, however. She often joined the other young people to picnic and play under an enormous weeping beech tree near Domremy.

"Sometimes I danced around the tree and sang," she said.

Joan also spent time praying in the church that was next door to her house. She was so devout that the young men often teased her.

Until she was thirteen, Joan lived quietly with her family. Then something happened that mystified her.

"It was summer," she said. "And I was in my father's garden. There appeared a great light around me."

In the light she saw a vision of Michael the Archangel, who told her to go to the aid of the King of France. In later visions, Saint Margaret and Saint Catherine also spoke to her.

France had been at war with England for many years. With the help of the French Duke of Burgundy, the English had taken over the northern half of the country. They even held the city of Rheims, where traditionally the King of France was crowned. Charles, who bore the title Dauphin because he was heir to the throne, could not be truly considered King of France until he was crowned in the cathedral at Rheims. But his coronation could not take place as long as the English controlled the city.

Joan's village had not been greatly troubled by the war until April 1428, three years after she first heard her voices. It was then that the Burgundian army attacked Domremy. Joan and her family fled with the other villagers. Returning after the raid, they found that the marauders had burned their church and other buildings.

Several months later, in October, the English and Burgundians surrounded the town of Orleans. By letting no food or supplies into the great walled city on the Loire River, they hoped to conquer it by starving the people. They thought that the rest of France would then surrender to them.

Joan's voices became insistent. They told her she must seek help from Robert de Baudricourt, the captain of the walled city of Vaucouleurs, near Domremy.

"Twice and three times a week, the voices told me I must raise the siege before Orleans," she said. "I told the voices that I was a poor girl who knew nothing of riding or warfare."

In spite of her reluctance, Joan, accompanied by an uncle, walked the twelve miles to Vaucouleurs. After refusing to help her several times, Robert de Baudricourt finally agreed to let Joan seek the Dauphin Charles at his castle in the city of Chinon.

Joan cropped her hair and changed from her red peasant dress into a man's tunic, hose, and leggings. Then she and six companions mounted their horses and set out for Chinon.

"I carried the sword that Robert de Baudricourt had given me," Joan said. "'Go,' he told me, 'and whatever may come of it, let it come.'"

After riding safely for eleven days through three hundred miles of enemy lands, Joan and her companions reached the Dauphin's castle on March 6, 1429. Joan entered the Dauphin's chambers. Charles, wanting to test her, to see if she would speak to the wrong person, had dressed less grandly than his courtiers and was mingling among them. Guided by her voices, Joan walked straight to him.

"Gentle Dauphin," she said, "I came on the behalf of the King of Heaven to raise the siege of Orleans and to conduct you to the cathedral at Rheims for your annointing and coronation."

Charles feared that she might be insane or a liar or even a witch. He turned her over to a church council for questioning.

"For three weeks I was examined by learned men," Joan said. "I was ill content with so much questioning."

The council found nothing wrong with her. Instead, Joan had convinced the members that she was Charles's only hope. They advised him to accept her help.

Charles finally agreed.

"I shall last a year and but little longer," she told the king. "We must think to do good work in that time."

The king sent her to the city of Tours, where she was joined by her brothers, Pierre and Jean. At Tours, she was given banners to carry into battle and fitted with a suit of brightly polished steel armor made especially for her. Although she had a sword, Joan's voices told her to send for an ancient sword buried behind the altar at Saint Catherine's Church in the town of Fierbois.

"The sword had rusted in the earth," she said. "The prelates of the church rubbed it, and at once the rust fell from it. It was as new."

From Tours she journeyed the thirty-six miles to Blois. There she raised an army and gathered supplies and food for the people of Orleans.

On April 27, 1429, Joan, as a captain with men under her command, set out for Orleans. Priests singing hymns led an army of six thousand soldiers, sixty wagons loaded with supplies, and four hundred cattle. They marched along the Loire River to Orleans, thirty-five miles away.

Joan rode up and down the lines of marchers, urging everyone to have faith and pray. On April 29, Joan led her army into the city of Orleans. Why the English did not stop her remains a mystery. The sound of clanging bells echoed through the city. The joyful people rushed into the streets to greet Joan as though she were an angel from God who had come to save them from starvation and death.

A few days later, on May 5, Joan sent a letter to the English.

"The King of Heaven orders you, through Joan the Maid, that you quit your fortresses and return to your own country," it read. "Or I shall raise such a war cry against you that it will be remembered forever."

She tied this message to an arrow, and a bowman shot it into the English lines.

The English laughed at her letter and shouted insults. Joan and her captains decided to wait no longer and attacked. During the next few days, they destroyed nine of the ten guard towers that the English had built around Orleans.

The English fled to the tenth and strongest tower. It blocked the only bridge across the Loire River into Orleans.

The next morning, Saturday, May 7, at seven o'clock, Joan led the attack against the tower.

Arrows rained down through the air. Cannons spit out wicked balls of chipped stones. Soldiers fought hand to hand with axes, lances, and clubs. During the battle, Joan seemed to be everywhere, encouraging the soldiers to fight for God and for France.

Early that afternoon, an arrow pierced her shoulder. She left the battlefield and pulled the arrow out with her own hands. After the wound was dressed with oil, she retired to a nearby vineyard to rest and pray.

The fighting went on until nearly eight o'clock that night. Doubting that they could win the battle, the French captains sounded the retreat. When Joan heard the trumpets, she left the vineyard and hurried back to rally the soldiers and lead them in one last charge.

"On! On!" she cried, waving her banner. "Do not fall back. This hour the English will be ours!"

When the English, who thought she was dead, saw that Joan had returned to the field of battle, they were terrified. They feared her more than any other French captain. Many believed she was a witch.

With Joan leading the way, the French regained their courage. They charged the tower and drove the English out.

The seven-month siege of Orleans was over.

Joan's victory at Orleans gave hope to the people of France. Hundreds of volunteers joined her army and drove the English from the towns surrounding Orleans.

Joan urged the Dauphin to go to Rheims to be officially crowned King of France. But Charles feared to travel through land still controlled by the English.

"Doubt not and fear nothing," Joan told him. "All will be well."

With her army, Joan led the way to Rheims, meeting little resistance from the English along the way. On Saturday, July 16, 1429, Joan and the Dauphin Charles entered Rheims. The next day, while her mother and father watched, Joan, with her banner, stood behind the Dauphin in the cathedral at Rheims as he was anointed and crowned King of France.

After the coronation, Joan wanted to free all of France from the English. But Charles refused to let Joan carry on the fight. He hoped to work out a peace treaty with the English. When the peace bargaining failed in April 1430, the king consented to Joan's request. She would fight the English again, though she was weary of battle.

"May it please God that I may soon put down my arms," she said, "and go serve my father and mother by keeping sheep with my sisters and brothers."

This time, however, there would be no victory. Charles had made a mistake. Over the months, he had sent many of his soldiers home, while the English had built up their army. Joan was wounded in a failed attempt to take Paris. When news of the defeat spread, many French nobles deserted Joan, although the peasants still had faith in her.

The end came on May 23 during a battle at Compiegne. A Burgundian archer grabbed Joan by her cloth-of-gold cloak. He dragged her from her horse and threw her to the ground. Joan the Maid, who had freed so many, was herself now a prisoner.

The Burgundian Duke Phillip demanded a ransom of ten thousand francs. Persuaded by his counselors, who were jealous of Joan, Charles decided that he had no further use for her. He refused to pay the ransom. The English, however, quickly did.

They persuaded the Catholic Church to try Joan as a heretic and a witch. The English bribed Pierre Cauchon, a French bishop friendly toward them, to hold the trial.

Joan was imprisoned in a castle tower for several months. Before she was brought to trial, she made an unsuccessful attempt to escape by jumping from the tower.

"I know that the English mean to put me to death," she said. "They think that after my death they will gain the Kingdom of France."

The trial began in Rouen on January 9, 1431. It was not conducted according to the usual rules. Joan had no lawyer or anyone to speak on her behalf. But she had her voices.

"There is no day that I do not hear them," she said at her trial. "I should be dead, were it not for their counsel that comforts me each day."

Bishop Cauchon secretly ordered the clerks who recorded Joan's testimony to alter what she had said. The trial dragged on for four months. Joan was found guilty, as she had predicted.

Bishop Cauchon turned her over to the sheriff of Rouen to carry out the sentence.

On Wednesday, May 30, 1431, Joan was brought to the marketplace and burned at the stake. Her ashes were cast into the River Seine. She was nineteen years old.

Most of the people who were there when she died knew that a great wrong had been done. Even the King of England's secretary wept.

"We are all lost," he cried. "We have burnt a good and holy person."

AUTHOR'S NOTE

Joan died before she freed France completely from the English. Some historians blame Charles, who, under the influences of traitorous counselors, deliberately delayed fighting the English for too long after he was crowned. After Joan's death, the English lost a good deal of their self-confidence. On the other hand, Charles, who had been so fearful, became filled with Joan's winning spirit. With the help of new advisors, many of whom had been Joan's strong supporters, he set out to fulfill the prediction Joan had made at her trial.

"Before seven years are done," she had said, "the English will lose more territory than they lost after losing Orleans."

Five years after Joan's death, on April 13, 1436, the French army freed Paris from the English. And within twenty-five years, the French had gained back all their country except for two cities, Bordeaux and Calais.

In 1450, Charles recaptured Rouen, the scene of Joan's trial. He then set about finding the truth. He soon discovered that Joan had been wrongly tried and condemned.

Guillaume Manchon, the notary at the trial, said, "When I set down the Maid's answers, sometimes the judge tried to have me put them in other terms, changing the meaning of the words."

On July 7, 1456, after a second trial, the archbishop of Rheims acknowledged that Joan's original trial had been wicked. Pope Calixtus III pronounced her innocent.

It wasn't until hundreds of years after her death, however, on May 9, 1920, that she was canonized by Pope Benedict XV. In July of that year, the French government proclaimed the day of her death, May 30, a national holiday in her honor.

In writing this biography, I depended on the letters, chronicles, and testimony presented at Joan's trial. The words of Joan that appear in the text are adapted from those records. My primary sources were *Joan of Arc: By Herself and Her Witnesses*, by Regine Pernoud, as translated by Edward Hyams from the French, and *Joan of Arc in Her Own Words,* compiled and translated by Willard R. Trask.